George Melville Baker

Rebecca's Triumph

A Drama

George Melville Baker

Rebecca's Triumph
A Drama

ISBN/EAN: 9783337345877

Printed in Europe, USA, Canada, Australia, Japan

Cover: Foto ©Thomas Meinert / pixelio.de

More available books at **www.hansebooks.com**

REBECCA'S TRIUMPH.

A Drama in Three Acts.

(FOR FEMALE CHARACTERS ONLY.)

WRITTEN EXPRESSLY FOR

"THE L. O. C. COOKING CLUB" OF CHICAGO.

BY

GEORGE M. BAKER.

BOSTON:
GEORGE M. BAKER AND COMPANY.
1879.

CHARACTERS.

MRS. ROKEMAN, a wealthy lady (age forty).
MRS. DELAINE, a widow (age sixty).
REBECCA, a foundling (age nineteen).
CLARISSA CODMAN, a spinster (age forty).
DORA GAINES,
SADIE MORRELL,
JENNIE WOODMAN,
MELLIE DUNBAR,
EMMA STEVENS, } Our Club.
GRACE GREENWOOD,
MARIA GRAY,
ALICE LEEDS,
GUSSIE GREEN,
KATIE CONNER, an Irish girl.
GYP, a colored girl.
MEG, a vagrant.

Time, three consecutive days in summer.

COSTUMES.

Mrs. Rokeman. Dark hair slightly streaked with gray or powdered. Different suits for the three acts, — walking, riding, and reception; all summer dresses.

Mrs. Delaine. Act I., calico dress, apron, gray wig, and cap. Act III., dark dress, light shawl, another cap and bonnet.

Rebecca and "Our Club." Suitable dresses for the kitchen, the grove, and the parlor, in the three acts, varied in colors and style.

Clarissa. Red hair front, with side ringlets; wrinkled face, highly colored; girlish dresses, with lace mantles, and broad-brimmed straw hat.

Katie. Red hair and calicoes.

Gyp. Woolley wig, black face, and black gloves for the hands; calico dress; turban for Acts II. and III.

Meg. Powder hair neatly; place over it a gray wig with long streaming hair. Wrinkle the face, but remove wrinkles before last appearance. Torn brown dress over a white skirt; arms bare. Drape a gray shawl by fastening the middle on waist L., then carry the ends to right shoulder and cross them, fastening there, ends hanging down before and behind.

3

REBECCA'S TRIUMPH.

ACT I.

SCENE. — MRS. DELAINE'S *kitchen, backed by garden scene. In flat* R. *large window reaching nearly to the floor; door* L. *in flat; screen standing* R., *back, behind which stove is supposed to be; door* R., *next screen; plain table against screen* R. *between door aud audience; door* L. *well up stage; plain table against scene on that side; plain table standing in* C.; *chairs near each table; white table-cloth over* C. *table, which* MRS. DELAINE *takes off and folds as curtain rises;* GYP *at table* R. *polishing a tin pan with a cloth; music at rising of the curtain.*

GYP. Dar, missus! (*holding up pan, and looking at the bottom as if it were a mirror.*) Dat ar bread-pan am got de polish. Now, let 'em talk about dar silber-white and dar stove-polish. Tęll yer what, missus! dar's nothin' like brack elbow-greese to gib de genuine lustre. Dat ar shines now jes like ole Daddy Brack's eyes when he got de lumbago, an' got 'em bad.

MRS. D. That's right, Gyp: make it shine. I want the cooking club to find every thing neat and tidy in my house.

GYP. Dar's no fear ob dat, missus: de little cookies will find ebery ting ready to upset, an' dey'll do dat shure's yer born. Mighty kind ob you, missus, to let 'em.

MRS. D. They are dear girls, with a laudable ambition to become good cooks; and, if I can assist them, it is not only a pleasure, but a duty. Is the fire burning briskly, Gyp?

GYP (*looking behind screen*). Red-hot, missus.

5

Mrs. D.   Fill the kettle and put it on.

Gyp.   Bress your soul, missus! it's dere now, buzzing like a bumble-bee.

Mrs. D.   That's well.   They will soon be here.

[*Exit with cloth, door* L.

Gyp (*comes to table, and takes up pan*).   Dar ain't no nonsense 'bout my missus, she's jes as good as gold; an' de goodness shines out ob her face brighter dan dis yere pan. An' dar's Miss Becky too, her 'dopted daughter, a born lady, dough she was picked up in de woods.   Ebery ting quiet and nice about de house.   Neber seed nuffin like it, an' I've lived round heaps.   (*Rubs pan.*)

(Katie *passes window, and stands in door.*)

Katie.   Is this the house I am afther huntin'?   (*Comes down to table* L.)   Is Mrs. Mouslin in, I dunno?

Gyp.   Missus, missus! — who's dat ar?

Katie.   Sure I said Mrs. Mouslin plain enough.

Gyp.   Dar's nobody here of dat name.   My missus am Missus Delaine.

Katie.   To be sure, Mrs. Delaine.   Faix! I knew it was some kind of a cloth.   Will, thin, I'm from the big house beyont, an' — an' I'm sint down wid a message.

Gyp.   Did — did you wipe your feet?

Katie.   Me fate, is it?   Sure, I'd not be demaning meself wiping me fate for a pine flure.   I'm from the big house, I tell yees.   I am quality, I am.

Gyp.   Don't want no white trash here, nor poor quality. Go away!

Katie.   I've come, and, bedad, it's not a black face will put me out of countenance, moind that, now!

Gyp.   I won't have nuffin to do wid yer: I won't asswotiate wid white help.

Katie.   Well. I'd loike to know if it's the Quane of Kamscatta, or the Prancess of Guiney yees are, onyhow, that yees so high-flown wid yer blarney.

Gyp.   Don't want nuffin to do wid yees.   Look at dar, look at dar!   (*Points to floor.*)   Dar's de prints ob yer hoofs on de clean floor.   (*Goes to screen, and brings out broom.*) Whare's your manners?   (*Sweeps about* Katie's *feet.*)

Katie (*snatching broom, and threatening* Gyp *with it*). Out of that, or I'll swape you out!   (Katie *moves to table* R.)

(*Enter* Mrs. D., *door* L.)

MRS. D. What's the matter here?

KATIE. A bit of a shindy, ma'am: that's all. I'm from the big house, if yer plase, ma'am.

GYP. Didn't wipe her feet.

MRS. D. Gyp, be quiet!

GYP. Brought in a heap of dirt.

MRS. D. Gyp!

GYP. Das a fac'. If I tole her fifty times, I tole her once, wipe her feet.

MRS. D. That's enough. Go into the wash-room: you will find plenty to do there.

GYP. Yas, missus. (*Turns up nose to* KATIE.) H'm! White trash! (*Exit door* R.)

MRS. D. Now, Katie, I will hear your message.

KATIÉ. Will, thin, if yees plase, ma'am, Mrs. Rokeman, my missus, axed me would I rin down to the fut of the hill, and ax Mrs. Mouslin (I mane Mrs. Delaine) would she be as kind and obleeging as to lend her the loan ov a twist.

MRS. D. Of what?

KATIE. Will, I don't know as I've just got that right. Och bother! You say Mrs. Delaine, Mrs. Rokeman, my missus, wants to take an airin' wid the fatone.

MRS. D. Mercy sakes! what do you mean?

KATIE. The little wagon, wid the clothes-basket onto it.

MRS. D. You mean a phaeton.

KATIE. Yes, ma'am. I'm obleeged to you. Will, there's not a man about the place the day, an' the whales are a little shaky; and she thinks, could she have a twist, I could tighten them.

MRS. D. I see: you want a wrench.

KATIE. Sure that's it. I knew it was some koind of an ache.

MRS. D. I'll lend her one with pleasure. (*Calls.*) Gyp. (*Enter* GYP.)

GYP. Yis, missus.

MRS. D. Take Katie Connor to the barn, and give her a wrench.

GYP. What! shake her, missus?

KATIE. I'd loike to see ye doing it.

MRS. D. The carriage-wrench, Gyp. Come, be lively.

GYP. Yis, missus. Come along, Miss Quality. (*Exit door* C.; *passes window, and exits* R.)

8   REBECCA'S TRIUMPH.

KATIE. I'm obleeged to yees. (*Courtesies, and exits after* GYP.)

MRS. D. Mrs. Rokeman ask a favor of me! the proud lady of the hill!—she who deigns not to notice her humble neighbors! Very strange!

(*Enter* REBECCA R. *behind window.*)

REBECCA (*at window*). Ah! good Mother Chirrup, here I am. (*Enter door.*) I've given the boys and girls a half-holiday, and it would just do your dear old heart good to see their merry faces: and I am just as ready for a frolic as they are. Nobody here yet?

MRS. D. None of your club, but I have had a visitor. Just think of it!—a message from the lady on the hill!

REBECCA. Mrs. Rokeman?

MRS. D. Yes. she has asked a favor of me; wanted to borrow. Think of that!—borrow of me!

REBECCA. Well, don't be proud, Mother Chirrup. Mrs. Rokeman might borrow from you many virtues which I fear she sadly lacks.

MRS. D. She only wanted a wrench, Becky, to fix the carriage.

REBECCA. Was that all?

MRS. D. That was all. Dear me! what a flutter it gives me, to be sure! And think of it! twenty years since we have spoken!

REBECCA. And you were her nurse? Shameful neglect!

MRS. D. Yes, twenty years ago Helen and Clara Delmar were handsome girls. Their father was a proud man: and, when Clara ran off with an artist, he disowned her; she has never been heard of since. Then Helen married Ralph Rokeman, a careless, good-for-nothing fellow, who broke his neck hunting in less than six months. Then Jasper Delmar died, and his widowed daughter has from that day to this lived solitary and alone in that grand old home.

REBECCA. And never made any attempt to find her sister?

MRS. D. Never, to my knowledge. On that matter we had bitter words, and parted. I came here, and we have never met since.

REBECCA. And here you would have lived as solitary and alone as the lady on the hill, had not your charitable doors and your kind heart opened to receive the waif of the woods.

MRS. D. Ah, Becky! Heaven sent you to be the comfort of my life.

REBECCA. I hope I am grateful, Mother Chirrup, for all your kindness to me. Eighteen years ago a dead man was found lying in the woods, with a living child, scarcely a year old, beside him. The guardians of the parish buried the dead stranger, and proposed sending the child to the poorhouse. But you, dear soul, took the child to your heart; and no mother could have cared more tenderly for her own than you have for me. Heaven bless you, Mother Chirrup! (*Throws her arms about* MRS. D.'*s neck.*)

MRS. D. Dear, dear me, Becky! You mustn't muss my cap; for you know we are to have company. (REBECCA *turns away.*) Don't talk about that time, child: it always makes you sad.

REBECCA. Is it strange? That man — who was he? Could he have been my father? Nothing about him to show who he was, or whence he came: nothing about me, save a ring suspended from my neck, — this (*points to finger*), — inside of which is engraved the one word " Remember."

MRS. D. Well, now, my child, it will all come out one of these days: if it doesn't, it is all the same. You have learned to take care of yourself; and, when I am gone, all I have is yours.

REBECCA. Dear Mother Chirrup! (*About to throw her arms about her.*)

MRS. D. Stop! stop! — my cap. You know I don't like to be hugged so. You are a dear good girl, Becky ; and, if I should lose you, it would break my heart. (*Throws her arms about* BECKY'S *neck, and sobs.*)

REBECCA (*kisses her*). Who's mussing now? (*Laughs.*) You don't like to be hugged ; but I do.

(MEG *appears at window.*)

MEG.
"We were two sisters of one race:
The wind is blowing in turret and tree."

That's right : make much of each other. You know not the day nor the hour when fate, cruel fate, shall break the bonds, and separate you forever. Ha, ha! I know, — I know. (*Enters at door. When she appears at window,* MRS. D. *and* REBECCA *separate* R. *and* L.)

MRS. D. Crazy Meg! Come in, Meg: you're always welcome here.

MEG. "Welcome!" I heard that word long years ago. 'Twas in a banquet-hall: the lights burned brightly; music filled the air. The bridegroom sat at the head of the table, and beside him the bride. Do you hear? the bride: 'twas I, Meg the outcast. Ha, ha! the bridegroom lifted high the brimming glass. A raven black as night sprang through the casement, dashed the glass from his hands, the lights went out, and I was left in darkness. The bridegroom — where is he? I can never find him, — never! (*Sinks into chair by table* R., *and buries her face in her arm.*)

MRS. D. Ah! there's a sad story there.

REBECCA (*lays her hand on* MEG'S *shoulder*). Cheer up, Meg: you are among friends.

MEG (*slowly lifting her head, and looking at* REBECCA). Ah! you are the schoolmistress. I've seen you with troops of girls and boys about you, with eager faces looking up at you. They love you; and I hunger for the sight of one little baby face that looked into mine, and smiled so sweetly! O baby, baby!

REBECCA. You, Meg? have you a child?

MEG (*quickly*). No, no! Who told you I had?

REBECCA. I understood you to say —

MEG. No, you cannot understand me: something's wrong here (*taps forehead*), so the doctors say. Don't mind me: I am only Meg, — crazy Meg.

REBECCA. Meg, you look tired and weary: this wandering life is killing you. That little hut in the woods is a loresome place. Come and live with us: you shall be made comfortable here. We have plenty of room, and would be glad to have you.

MEG. You cannot mean it, pretty face. I am old and ugly: your neat home will be disfigured by my presence. No, no! let me wander.

REBECCA. You know not how tender care will transform you. (*Kneels at her side.*) Look at me, Meg! I was once as poor as you. When a little child, I was left alone in the wild woods to die.

MEG (*staring at her*). You?

REBECCA. Yes, I: no mother, no father; no one in the wide world to claim me or care for me. But that good woman

there took the strange, forsaken one to her arms, as she will
now take you, poor outcast.

MEG (*looks at her eagerly*). Alone in the woods!—you?
(*Starts to her feet.*) Oh, let me go from here quick! Your
face, your words, shape far-off memories that they told me I
must forget, or I should go mad,—mad. (*Crosses to* L.)

MRS. D. Meg, you must be hungry: let me get you something to eat.

MEG. No, no! I cannot eat.

REBECCA. A cup of tea?

MEG. No, no! I must have air!—air! (*Goes up totter-
ing.* REBECCA *puts her arm about her waist.*)

REBECCA. You are faint and ill. You shall not go until
you are rested. Come. everybody in this house obeys me,
and so must you.

MEG (*looks up in her face*). You've a kind heart, pretty
face. Somewhere in the future you'll be the light of a
happy home. Do with me as you will. There's something
in your face calms me, overcomes me. (*Kisses her hand.*)
I am your slave forever. (*Music.* REBECCA *slowly leads
her off door* L.)

MRS. D. That's a wonderful girl: I must say it, if I did
have the bringing of her up. She's mastered every thing
she sets about; and, last of all, wild Meg, who's been
such a roaming vagabond round here for the last six
months! Nobody knows who she is, or where she comes
from; but, if Becky don't find out before she's done with her,
I'm mistaken.

(*Enter* GYP *by window, through door.*)

GYP. Missus, de cookies am coming:. heard 'em on de
hill, laughing and singing like a Mefodis' camp-meeting.
Precious little work dey'll do dis yer aternoon.

(*Chorus outside. Air, "Nancy Lee."*)

The kitchen-fire does brightly glow,
You know, girls, know, you know, you know;
The shining pans hang in a row,
You know, girls, know, you know;
And all is neat and snug and sweet
For you and me
To brew and bake, to mould and make,
Or frolic free.
Our happy day will pass away
With mirth and glee,

You know, girls, know, you know;
The dainty dish the maiden's pride shall be.
You know, we go, to work with glee.
The dainty dish the maiden's pride'shall be;
The dainty dish our pride shall be.

(*When the song reaches "The dainty dish the maiden's pride," &c., the singers appear behind window, finish it, and then with a laugh flock into the kitchen-door as follows,—* DORA, SADIE, JENNIE, MELLIE, EMMA, GRACE, MARIA, ALICE, *and* GUSSIE. MRS. D. *is near table* R.; GYP *at table left.*)

DORA (*running up to* MRS. D., *and taking both hands with a vigorous shake*). How d'ye do, Mother Chirrup? Here we are, you see. (*Crosses to* GYP.) How d'ye do, Gyp? (*All follow her example; make it lively.*)

MRS. D. Glad to see you, girls: we are all ready for you.

GYP. Das a fac'.

DORA. Of course you are; and, if· I'm not mistaken, you'll be glad to see the last of us. You heard my new song? Original, — quite original. Words and music both my own, — a musical cake made out of my own head.

GIRLS (*in chorus*). O Do! (*Laugh.*)

DORA. No: there is no dough about it.

GYP. Den how could yer make it out ob your own head? (*Girls laugh.*)

DORA. O Gyp! how could you! Come, girls: off with your hats, and on with your aprons. (*Girls take off hats, and pile them on* GYP'S *arms; then each one takes apron from pocket and puts it on, talking together.* GYP *carries hats off door* L.; *then some of the girls sit in the chairs, others behind them.*)

SADIE. What's the programme?

MRS. D. Becky will be here in a moment. (*Exit door* L.)

NELLIE. Becky is mistress to-day.

EMMA. I'm glad of that: she always has some new dish.

MARIA. She'll want more new dishes when we are gone. (*Girls laugh.*)

DORA. Yes, if we undertake to make pumpkin-pies, as we did at your house.

SADIE. When Maria and Jennie undertook to put the pies in the oven —

DORA. And their heads came.together: the pumpkin-

pies were transformed to squash (*girls laugh*) and turn-
overs. (*Laugh.*)

MARIA. I couldn't help it. The floor was slippery, and
the time short.

DORA. But the pie-crust wasn't. (*Laugh.*) Here's Becky.
(*Enter* REBECCA, *door* L.) Hail to the chief — cook! How
d'ye do, Becky? (*All flock about her, with how d'ye-does,
hand-shakes, and hugs.*)

REBECCA. Don't smother me, girls!

DORA. Well, here we are, armed and equipped as the
law of cooking directs. What is it? — pies, cakes, or fancy
dishes? A dainty dish for me. (*All sing last part of song.*)

" The dainty dish," &c.

REBECCA. Suppose we try cake to-day. I've found a
nice receipt among Mrs. Miller's " In the Kitchen " (*shows
book*), — " Rebecca's Triumph."

GIRLS (*in chorus*). Good! let's have it. Read it, Becky.

REBECCA (*reads*), " Rebecca's Triumph," — " Half a pound
of butter, one and a quarter pounds of sugar, eighteen ounces
of flour, one ounce of blanched almonds cut in strips, one
ounce of raisins stoned, half a pint of milk, one and a half
tablespoonfuls of baking-powder sifted into the flour, six
eggs; cream the butter, and add the sugar gradually, with a
little of the milk, to make them mix; beat the whites and
yolks together until light, then stir them into the butter and
sugar; add the rest of the milk and the flour, then the
almonds and raisins. Bake in loaves." There it is: shall
we try it?

DORA. Of course. Those in favor of trying " Rebecca's
Triumph " say " Ay!"

GIRLS. Ay!

DORA. 'Tis a unanimous vote.

GUSSIE. You didn't count the noes, Do.

DORA. Yours wouldn't count, Gussie, if it was called:
it's too small. " Rebecca's Triumph:" there's something
high-toned in the name, and, as Becky is to be the manager
of this occasion, very appropriate. Come, Becky: give your
orders, and we'll get to work.

REBECCA. You all know where to find things in this
house. First for eggs, the freshest and best. Alice and
Maria will find them in the barn (*exeunt by door* ALICE

and MARIA, *who pass window*). Grace will look after the butter and sugar (GRACE *runs off door* R.); Sadie, the milk (SADIE *passes out of door-flat, passes window*); Jennie and Mellie, the flour and baking-powder (JENNIE *and* MELLIE *exeunt door* R.). Emma will take care of the raisins, and Gussie will look after the tins (EMMA *and* GUSSIE *exeunt door* R.). There, I believe all are set to work.

DORA. Except me.

REBECCA. You, Dora, may blanch the almonds.

DORA. All right. (*Takes* BECKY'S *hand*.) That's a pretty ring you wear. I never noticed it before.

REBECCA.– 'Tis very dear to me.

DORA. It's too large for your finger. Take care, or you'll lose it some day. (*Exit* R.)

REBECCA. Lose it. No, no! 'Tis all I have to unite me with the past,––that mysterious past, whose darkness I sometimes think will be dispelled by this ring, with its motto "Remember." I know not why it was hung about my neck: but something long ago told me it was my mother's; that she must be dead, or she would not have parted with it; that its motto tells of loving vows, and hopes of happiness, perhaps blasted by misfortune. To me it is very precious. (*Kisses it.*) "Remember." Yes, mother, though we may never meet on earth, by this token you are ever near and dear to me. (*Exit door* L.) (*Lively music.* GUSSIE *runs on from door* R. *with an earthen dish for mixing; places it on table* C., *then runs off door* R. DORA *runs on from door* R. *with almonds in dish; places it on table* L., *then runs behind screen* R. GUSSIE *runs on with bowl and cups for breaking and beating the eggs; also beater; places them on table* R., *and runs off door* R. ALICE *and* MARIA *run on behind, past window, in at door, down to table* L., *and break and beat the eggs.* GRACE *runs on door* L. *with butter and sugar; goes to table* C., *and creams butter, and adds sugar.* SADIE *runs on from outside with milk, and assists.* GUS-SIE *runs to* C. *table, and helps.* JENNIE *runs on from door* L. *with flour and sifter, and sifts flour at table* R. EMMA *brings on raisins from door* R.; *sits near* R. *table, and stones raisins. All lively, chatter and talk, if they please. Music, pianissimo, so the voices can be heard. Enter* GYP *door* L.)

GYP. Bress my soul! it am as busy here as a barbecue. (*Crosses to table* R.) Miss Jennie, let me do dat: dat's no kind of work for your lily fingers.

JENNIE (*takes her hand out of the flour, and lays it on* GYP'S *cheek, leaving it white.*) No, I thank you, Gyp: it whitens them, don't you see?

GYP (*wiping his face*). Don't do dat, chile: folks'll tink 1 powder.

DORA (*behind screen*). Clear the way; for I am coming. (*Appears with tea-kettle; crosses stage to table* L.)

GYP (*coming to table* L.). Dat's too heaby for you, Miss Dora. Let me do dat. (*Just as she reaches table, and puts out her hand,* DORA *pours boiling water on almonds.*) Oh, massy sakes, you've burnt me! (*Holds her hand, and dances about stage. Music stops.*)

DORA (*carrying the kettle back behind screen*). Sorry, Gyp; but children should never put their fingers into the sugar-bowl without leave.

GYP (*blowing her hand*). Oh! she's smart, she is. But dar's going to be trouble here. If dey don't blow de roof off afore dey gits frough, den you can call me Misstook. I'll jes put myself out ob de way. (*Exits door* C., *and passes window.*)

DORA (*returns to table, singing*).

Air, "*Oh! give me a Cot in the Valley I love.*"

Oh! give me a place in the kitchen I love,
A cake in the oven, a fire in the stove,
I care not how heavy, contented I'll be,
If some one will eat it when cookèd by me.

(*Girls laugh.*)

JENNIE. Come, Mellie: hurry with the baking-powder.

(*Enter* MELLIE *with a bottle and knife; something in the bottle to fly, — soda or mineral-water.*)

MELLIE. Can't find the powder. Here's a bottle of yeast: won't that do? (*Cuts string; cork flies; all scream. Some jump on chairs; while* MELLIE *flies around, and tries to stop the fermentation with her hands.*)

JENNIE. You careless thing! that won't do at all. (*Enter* REBECCA *door* L.)

REBECCA. What's the matter? (*takes bottle from* MEL-LIE.) You want the baking-powder: I'll find it. (*Exit door* R.)

JENNIE. Well, Mellie Dunbar, I hope you're satisfied now. See what a mess you've made!

DORA. Yes, Mellie's made a melancholy failure. (*Enter* REBECCA *with baking-powder.*)

REBECCA. Here it is, Mellie (*gives her box : she goes to table* R.). Now let me see how you are getting along (*goes from one to the other*).

(CLARISSA *appears at door in flat.*)

CLARISSA (*with an affected drawl*). Why, how de do, girls? Hard at work? This is delightful; pos-i-tively charming!

DORA. Mercy! there's the old maid! Now won't we catch it!

REBECCA. Ah! good afternoon, Miss Codman. Walk in.

CLARISSA. Thank you. (*Enters and comes* C., *looking about with an eyeglass.*) So domestic! It reminds me of my early days, when I used to make dirt-pies in my little garden with my little brother.

DORA. I don't see how you can remember that : it must have been years and years ago.

CLARISSA. Oh, no! I have not yet lost the springing steps of girlhood, the rosy dreams of youth. My gentle heart thrills at the passionate appeals of the lover in my reading, and I grow brave at the daring exploits of the heroine of romance. I feel as if I could do brave deeds myself, — "beard the lion in his den, the Douglas in his hall."

DORA (*screams, and jumps upon chair*). A mouse, a mouse! (*Girls scream, and gather their skirts about them.* MELLIE *sits on table, and others jump on chairs.* CLARISSA *runs down to* L. *corner, opens her parasol, and points it at the floor.*)

REBECCA (*comes* C.). Nonsense, girls! Where did you see it, Dora?

DORA (*jumps from chair*). "In my mind's eye, Horatio."

JENNIE. You hateful thing!

SADIE. You ought to be ashamed of yourself! (*Girls resume work.*)

DORA. I couldn't help it. Miss Codman looked so brave, that I wanted to scare up some game for her.

CLARISSA. Oh, a joke! Ha, ha! A joke! Girls are so sportive! (*Aside*) I'd like to shake the hussy!

DORA (*hands chair*). Take a seat, Miss Codman : you're all of a tremble.

CLARISSA (*sits in corner*). Thank you. Don't let me in-
terrupt your delicious pastime, it is so conducive to health,
so useful as a preparation for that domestic life which must
come to us all at last. (*Sighs*) Heigh-ho!
JENNIE. I wonder if she expects it to come to her.
MELLIE. While there is life, there is hope.
CLARISSA. I have just been to the post-office. I found a
letter awaiting me, a tender epistle, from you know who,
Rebecca, — my mysterious correspondent, Theophilus Montague.
REBECCA. I remember you told me you had received a
note from an unknown correspondent. I also remember I
advised you to treat it with contempt.
CLARISSA. I could not do that. It was so respectful, so
eloquent of sincere admiration, so tremulous with suppressed
passion, that I fell into the epistolary snare set to capture my
sensitive and susceptible heart. I answered it with tender
lines, that fed the flame of love; and he writes again, so
sweet, so tender! (*Kisses paper.*) Do let me read you a
few lines.
CHORUS OF GIRLS. Oh, do, do, do!
CLARISSA (*opens note, and reads*). "Charming Clarissa!"
GIRLS (*in chorus*). Oh, splendid!
CLARISSA (*reads*). "Your dainty epistle has reached me.
It now reposes near my heart, adding fuel to the fire that
flames within me."
DORA. Won't the oven get too hot?
(GRACE *runs behind screen, then returns to table.*)
CLARISSA (*looks around, then reads*). "It needs but one
thing more to make it rise" —
JENNIE *to* MELLIE. A little more baking-powder!
CLARISSA (*looks around, then reads*). "Like the fabled
phœnix from its ashes, to soar to the Elysium of your love."
DORA. That's too lovely for any thing!
(REBECCA *goes to table*, C., *to mix the cake. Stands behind
it.*)
CLARISSA (*reads*). "What can I bring you, dearest," —
REBECCA. Eggs, Alice! (ALICE *carries the beaten eggs
to* REBECCA.)
CLARISSA. Eggs: oh! excuse me. (*Reads*) "To obtain
the one thing I desire," —
REBECCA. Flour, Jennie! (JENNIE *carries flour to* RE-
BECCA.)

CLARISSA (*irritated*). "Your sweet consent to our wedding nuptials. I have no gold; but I have" —
REBECCA. A little more milk, Sadie!
CLARISSA. Oh, this is mockery!
DORA. Oh, go on, go on! It's splendid!
GIRLS (*in chorus*). Lovely! Go on, go on!
CLARISSA. "A heart, and in that heart are" —
REBECCA. Raisins, Emma! (EMMA *carries raisins*.)
CLARISSA. Oh! (*desperately*.) "High hopes and" —
REBECCA. Almonds, Dora! (DORA *carries up almonds. The girls are all about table, watching* REBECCA, *and forgetting* CLARISSA.)
CLARISSA (*desperately*). "High hopes and noble aspirations*" (*waits for an exclamation: all silent. She slowly turns round, and looks at the girls; then folds the note, and puts it in her bosom*). This is "wasting sweetness on the desert air." I'll go home, and in the silence of my chamber brood over the love-lit words from the flowery pen of passion. O my Theophilus! unseen, unknown, but not unloved. No more your precious missives are to be intrusted to the prying eyes of the plebeian post-mistress. You have named a trysting-tree in the gloomy forest, within whose hollow trunk henceforth our epistolary messages of love are to nest themselves. I will remember. and to-morrow convey my answer to its oaken keep. (*Straightens up, puts parasol under her arm, and marches up to door in flat, and off, past window*.)
REBECCA. Now, Gussie, we are all ready for the pans. (GUSSIE *runs off* R.) Miss Codman, go on, if you please.
DORA (*turns around*). Go on. She's gone off!
GIRLS (*turn around*). Oh, that's too bad!
JENNIE (*comes down* R.). I wanted to hear the last of that letter.
DORA. Did you? So you shall. I know every word in it; for I wrote it. I am (*puts her thumbs. as a man would in the arm-holes of his vest, and struts down to* JENNIE) Theophilus Montague.
JENNIE. What! you, Dora?
            (GUSSIE *enters door* R *with the cake-pans*.)
DORA. Yes; and I've had such fun! She really believes that some mysterious individual, who, on account of his poverty, is afraid to seek an introduction, has taken this ro-

mantic way of making his affection known. Oh, if you could
only read her epistles!—such gushing moonshine, such
ridiculous nonsense! But I wouldn't show them for the
world. You know we are to have a picnic to-morrow in the
grove; and, to give a little fun to the occasion, I have con-
trived to make a post-office of the old oak. So to-morrow, if
you don't see fun, then my name is not Dora Gaines.

REBECCA. One loaf is ready, Dora. Will you put it in
the oven?

DORA. Yes, indeed. (*Goes up to table, takes pan, and
carries it behind screen.*)

GYP (*outside*). O missus! missus! here's trubble! (*Runs
in door* C.)

REBECCA. What's the matter, Gyp?

GYP. Let me get my breff. Dat lady up to de house on
the hill is jest runnin' away down de road. One wheel off
de hub, and she jest hangin' on, an' dat are horse flyin'!

REBECCA (*runs to door*). It's Mrs. Rokeman (*runs off* R.
by the window).

GYP. Bress my soul! She's nebber goin' to try to stop
dat ar horse! Break her neck, sure! (GIRLS *run off behind
window, and stand looking off* R. GYP *stands at door, with
hand shading her eyes, looking off* R.)

DORA (*runs out, by* GYP, *among the* GIRLS). Who is it?
Where is it? What is it?

JENNIE. Mrs. Rokeman's horse is running away, and I
do believe Becky's going to try and stop him!

DORA. Of course she is. See! she has reached the
horse! She is running with it! Now her hand is on the
bridle: still she runs. Now she draws it tight. He's drag-
ging her from her feet. No: his pace slackens. She has
him now! Bravo, Becky!

GIRLS (*clap their hands*). Bravo, bravo!

DORA. She's all right now. Mercy! my cake! (*Runs in
and behind screen; girls return.*)

GYP (*at door*). She's a bringin' dat ar lady here. Speck
I'd better look arter de horse. (*Exit past window* R. GIRLS
carry off pans, &c., door R. *Pan with one loaf of cake left
on table* C. *Enter, passing by window, and through door,*
REBECCA, *with her arm about* MRS. ROKEMAN, *whose
hand is on her shoulder; seats her in chair near table* C. A
little music while this is going on.)

REBECCA.   You are safe now, madam.

MRS. R.   Thanks to you, my dear girl.   You have saved my life.   My wheel slipped off on the hill, and frightened the horse.   My hold on the phaeton was relaxing.   In another moment I should have been hurled out upon the rocky road.   Mine is but a worthless life.   I have prayed for death many and many a night; but, when it was so near me, I felt how dear and precious life is.

REBECCA.   I am glad I have been of service.   But I think you overrate the danger.   The carriage is low, and a slip into the road would have been a frolic to me.

MRS. R.   Ah! you are young and happy; you have become strong by exercise: while I am weak and timid. The shock and the fear would have killed me.   How can I repay you?

REBECCA.   By saying nothing more about it.   I shall begin to think I am a heroine, if you make so much of a simple affair.   (*Girls return; some come down* R., *others pass to* L.)   Why, any of our club would have done the same, and thought nothing of it: wouldn't you, girls?

DORA (R.).   Speak for yourself, Becky.   There's not another girl in our club brave enough to think of any thing but screaming at sight of a runaway horse.

JENNIE (L.).   I guess not: catch her near a horse's heels!

SADIE.   We should all run the other way: wouldn't we, girls?

CHORUS OF GIRLS.   Yes, indeed!

MRS. ROKEMAN.   May I ask what "our club" is?

DORA.   A cooking-club, Mrs. Rokeman.   We've been experimenting to-day with one of Becky's receipts for cake. She calls it "Becky's Conquest."

GIRLS (*laugh*).   O Dora!

DORA.   No: "Rebecca's Triumph."   And I know it's just splendid.   You see, we visit each other's homes, anywhere we are invited.

MRS. R.   Indeed!   Then allow me to extend a cordial invitation to "our club" to visit my home.   I am a lonely woman, and the sight of your merry faces in my house would be a pleasure to me.

GIRLS.   Oh! thank you.

REBECCA.   I fear we should intrude.   We are a noisy set when allowed our liberties.

MRS. R. The more noise, the better. I should like to taste your cake.

DORA (R.). It's cooking now. It won't be nice to eat to-day.

MRS. R. Then suppose you set a day to visit me, and bring me a morsel of your cake. Let me see. This is Tuesday. Suppose we say Thursday. Would that be agreeable?

GIRLS. Oh, yes!—splendid!

MRS. R. Then we will consider it settled.

REBECCA. O girls! my ring! I've lost my ring! I must have dropped it in the road.

DORA. I'll go and find it. (*Goes up to door.*)

JENNIE. So will I. (*Follows.*)

GIRLS. We'll all go. (*Trip out of door, and past window, singing,—*

"A dainty dish, the maiden's pride," &c.)

REBECCA (*comes down* R.; MRS. ROKEMAN *watches her*). Oh! if it should be lost! Without it, now, I feel as if part of my life had gone from me.

MRS. R. (*rises, and comes down*). I have been watching you, child. Something in your face is strangely familiar. Have we ever met before?

REBECCA. Not to my knowledge.

MRS. R. Who are you?

REBECCA. The schoolmistress in the place,—the adopted daughter of Mrs. Delaine.

MRS. R. My old nurse! Where is she?

(*Enter* MRS. D., *door* L.)

MRS. D. Here, Mrs. Rokeman!

MRS. R. Mary, my dear old nurse! (*Holds out hands.*) Can you forgive me?

MRS. D. (*takes hands, and presses them warmly*). I have nothing to forgive, Miss Helen.

MRS. R. My neglect?

MRS. D. Don't speak of it! We parted in anger twenty years ago. You thought you was right, and I knew I was. With so strong a difference of opinion, we could scarcely remain friends; and, if I cannot have friends, I wish no acquaintances.

MRS. R. Still obstinate, I see!

MRS. D. On that point, yes. I told you you did not treat your sister fairly, and twenty years have not changed that opinion.

MRS. R. (*proudly*). Neither have they mine. My sister left her happy home to follow an adventurer, with no legal right to bear his name.

MRS. D. That's false! He was her husband.

MRS. R. Have you any proof of that?

MRS. D. The best. Her birth, her education, her true and noble heart, — all proofs of her goodness, virtue, and truth.

MRS. R. I want stronger proof. No distance would have separated her from her home forever; no circumstances shut out the love from her heart, save shame.

MRS. D. Have you sought for proofs?

MRS. R. No.

MRS. D. Is she living, or dead?

MRS. R. I do not know. I have not dared to search, lest my worst suspicions should be realized. Heaven knows I loved her, — love her still; but ours is a proud name, and no blot of shame shall ever tarnish it while I live. No more of this. Your adopted daughter has done me a great service. I would befriend her. Give her to me. I will be a mother to her, and, should she prove worthy, make her my heiress.

MRS. D. What! my Becky heiress to the grand estate, the Delmar name? Do you hear, Becky?

REBECCA. I hear.

MRS. D. Why, here's a brilliant future for you, Becky! Heiress! — why, Becky, I never dreamed of such good fortune!

MRS. R. Rebecca, will you go with me?

REBECCA (*quietly*). Thank you, no. I am happy here, — my own mistress, and quite content.

MRS. D. Becky, you are mad to refuse such an offer.

BECKY. Do you think so? My happiest days have been spent in this dear home. The first, best love of life, a mother's, I have found in your dear heart. There is nothing sweeter, purer, better, in this world, than that. (*Throws her arms about* MRS. D.) You have won me: you shall keep me.

MRS. D. (*hugging* BECKY). I knew I should, my Becky! Oh, I'm a happy old woman!

MRS. R. (*turns to* R. *aside*). Oh, how I envy them! From my lonely habitation, rich in all that wealth can purchase, I can look out on broad lands stretching far, o'er fields and woodlands, beautiful in fruits and ripening grain, and call them mine. Yet here's a simple girl, whose love I covet, turns away from all that might be hers to homely life with all its cares, — contented, happy in the love that nursed her into life. Oh, I am poor indeed! (*Sinks into chair near table* R., *and covers her face with her hands.*)

Song outside L. MEG. Air, "Tired."

> Sisters were we, yes, sisters true,
>   In our old happy home :
> No saddening shadows then we knew ;
>   And now I lonely roam.
> I'm longing to meet, yes, meet again, —
>   Longing for her embrace :
> The glooming shadows fall again,
>   Forever to hide her face.

(*During the singing* MRS. R. *looks up and about her, very much affected.* REBECCA *stands* L. *with* MRS. D., *their arms about each other, listening.*)

MRS. R. Who is that singing? Whose voice? Tell me quick!

REBECCA. That is wild Meg, as she is called, — a poor half-crazy wanderer, whom I have put to rest in my room.

MRS. R. Wild Meg! But that voice! those words! I must see her (*rises*) at once (*goes towards door* L.).

(*Enter* MEG *door* L. *Chord. They stand and look at each other.*)

MRS. R. (*stepping back*). No: this is the face and form of an old woman. It was the song which deceived me.

MEG. Deceived! Have you been deceived? So have I. Ha, ha! You are rich and proud, — rings on your fingers, jewels in your ears ; and I'm in rags. Yet we are sisters.

MRS. R. (*agitated*). How? — what mean you?

MEG (*points up*). In the sight of Heaven, rich and poor, high and low, brothers and sisters all, sent to love, but remain to hate each other! I could tell you a story, lady, of two sisters, that would make your heart bleed with pity. They were rich ; but one married a poor man. The father disowned her ; and the sister, when the riches became hers, forgot her, for fear she might come and claim her share.

MRS. R. No, no! 'Tis false! She had no such motive.

MEG. Ah! you know her?

MRS. R. It is my own story, which you have picked up in your wanderings about here. Be careful, woman! There is more of cunning than madness in you; and, if you prate of my affairs, I'll have you locked up where your ravings will not be heard. Remember!

MEG (*starts*). Remember (*aside*): no, no! (*Aloud.*) Remember you!—there will come a time when your proud head shall lie in the dust. Cunning!—yes, so cunning, that I could tell you the two sisters loved one man. They pledged each other that his choice should be sacred: pledged each other with rings. No matter what came: their love for each other should continue. He chose the younger, and the sister —

MRS. R. Woman, who are you?

MEG. One who never did you wrong: one who from the stars obtains secrets; who hopes for justice, prays for justice, and so is mad!—ha, ha!—mad, mad!

(*Exit by door* C. *to* L.)

MRS. R. From the stars? No, no! this woman is an emissary of my sister, trusted with secrets of ours, and sent to goad me into madness. She shall be driven from the place. (*Talks with* REBECCA L.)

GIRLS (*outside*). Ha, ha, ha!

DORA (*outside*). Come along: it's no use to search any more. (*Enter* DORA *and others door* R. *Come down* R. *and* L.) Becky, the ring is not in the road: you must have dropped it about the house.

REBECCA. Then it's sure to be found: so give yourselves no more trouble. Have you looked at the cake, Dora?

DORA. Goodness gracious, the cake! (*runs behind screen.*)

MRS. R. (*to* REBECCA). I'm sorry you cannot come and live with me; but you will come often and see me?

REBECCA. Thank you, if it will please you.

MRS. R. I shall expect to see you all on Thursday, and that wonderful cake.

DORA (*appears from behind screen with pan, in which is a very black cake*). The cake can't come: it's gone into mourning.

JENNIE. Completely ruined!

GIRLS. Oh, dear!

MRS. D. (*lifting her hands*). , Well done!

DORA. Yes, it is well done, — over-done.

REBECCA. No matter: we've another loaf.

DORA. Thank Goodness for that.

MRS. R. You will find a warm welcome awaiting you at Delmar. It will be red-letter day in my lonely life. Do not disappoint me. (MEG *passes door from* L.) Remember!

MEG (*at window*). Remember! — ha, ha! Gather the young and merry about you; seek to banish the bitter past. Your efforts are vain. Out of shadows points a skeleton finger, and in your blasted heart is imprinted in letters of fire one word, — " Remember! "

(MRS. R. *sinks into chair right of table* C.; MRS. D. *runs to her, and stands behind chair;* REBECCA *kneels, and takes her hand, looking up at her face; girls grouped* R. *and* L.; MEG *behind window, with finger pointing at* MRS. R. *Soft music, slow Curtain.*)

END FIRST ACT.

ACT II.

THE PICNIC. SCENE. — *A grove ; flat a wood ;* C., *three feet from back, set tree with branches reaching over and into side-scene* R., *forming an arch ; same on left, but a wider opening ; at* R., *tree with hollow trunk, bank ;* L. *rustic. bench, before* C. *tree ; swing hung behind opening ;* R. C. *to swing ;* R. *and* L. *past opening ; chorus ; commence a little before rising of the curtain ; then rise on picture.* RE-BECCA *seated on bench* C. ; JENNIE *seated on stage beside her, with her arm thrown across* REBECCA'S *lap ;* SADIE *in the swing, singing ;* GRACE *on bench* L. ; MELLIE *standing behind her, placing flowers in her hair ;* DORA *leaning against tree* R. ; MARIA *swinging* SADIE ; EMMA *seated near* DORA, *making a band of leaves ;* ALICE *and* GUSSIE, *their arms about each other's waists, stand* L. C. *opening.*

(*Chorus.   Air, " There's Music in the Air."*)

I.

There's beauty in the grove
When the opening Spring, unseen,
With fairy touch invests
All the earth with robes of green ;
While the birds' exultant song
All the rocks and woods prolong :
Then all hearts are filled with love
For the beauty of the grove.

II.

There's beauty in the grove
When the Summer's sultry air
Commands a safe retreat
To its cool and mossy lair,

With its wealth of bloom arrayed,
Fragrant breath and grateful shade:
All enchanted there we rove
'Mid the beauty of the grove.

III.

There's beauty in the grove
When the Autumn's magic spell
Transforms with dainty touch
All the glowing, leafy dell.
Yellow, red, and brown combine,
Golden lustre's quivering shine;
Then we joy all else above
In the beauty of the grove.

DORA. Oh, I'm so hungry!

JENNIE. That's complimentary, I declare, after the musical feast we have just spread before you!

DORA. Music, like other tonics, only creates an appetite for food.

JENNIE. Music is food, so Shakspeare says, — "the food of love."

DORA. Oh, yes! Love can feed on air or moonshine, and music is quite as unsubstantial. That's why lovers always look so pale and thin. I'm not in love, and I'm awful hungry!

JENNIE. Awful, Dora? Then these old trees should satisfy that hunger. Don't the poets say they fill one with awe? (*Girls laugh.*)

DORA. O Jennie Woodman, spare that tree. Are we ever going to get any thing to eat?

JENNIE. "In the sweet by-and-by." I declare, Dora, you quite destroy the romance of this lovely solitude with such earthly longings. Doesn't she, girls?

CHORUS OF GIRLS. Yes, indeed!

JENNIE. I could roam these woods for days, breathing the odor of the pines, feasting my eyes on the verdure, plucking the beautiful flowers, and never grow weary or faint. It's just lovely, isn't it, girls?

GIRLS (*in chorus*). Perfectly lovely.

DORA. Indeed! And yet you girls are all just as hungry as I am.

CHORUS OF GIRLS. Oh, no!

DORA (*comes* C.). Here comes Gyp with the basket.

GIRLS (*all flock about* DORA). Oh, good, good! The basket — where is it?

DORA. "In the sweet by-and-by."

GIRLS (*turn away*). Oh!

DORA. Now, don't feel bad: you've got the piney odors,
and the variegated verdure, and the beautiful flowers. Just
lovely, isn't it, girls?

JENNIE. Dora, how could you?

GRACE. You're just awful!

MELLIE. Ought to be ashamed of yourself!

GIRLS (*in chorus*). O Dora!

DORA. There's a chorus of hungry mouths.

REBECCA (*seated*). I'm very sorry, girls. Gyp was to
have started from the house an hour ago with the basket.

JENNIE. What can have become of her?

DORA. Lost her way; perhaps wandering like a black •
babe in the woods. I move that we appoint a committee of
the whole to go in search of the black diamond.

GIRLS. Oh! let's.

DORA. Unanimous vote. Follow me.   •

> We'll scour the woods, and o'er the mountains skip,
> Until we find the long-lost dusky Gyp.

Come along.

(*Girls march once around in the stage in couples after*
DORA, *then off* L. *opening by trees, and exit* R., *singing one
stanza of*

> "There's beauty in the grove.")

REBECCA (*after the chorus has died away in the distance*).
I wonder how long it will be before they miss me. There's
no false pride about our girls. As freely and warmly as my
love goes out to them, as freely and warmly it is returned.
Never a word or look of scorn for the poor charity-girl.
Poor! — I blush at the thought. Am I not honored, re-
spected, beloved? Yesterday I might have been envied by
them all. Mrs. Rokeman, without a question, would have
taken me to her heart. Why was this, something in my face?
I am not beautiful. What can it be? It has awakened the
old longing for knowledge of the past. How often in solitude have I sat and looked at the old tree fast fading to
decay, which, if it had the power of speech, might tell me
something of my history!

DORA (*outside*). Becky!
GIRLS (*in chorus*). Becky!
REBECCA (*rises; goes to tree* R.). Beneath its shade a
weary man laid himself down to die, with me, a prattling
child, clasped in his arms. Was he a pitiless wretch, who
had snatched me from my cradle? or was he a tender father
bearing me from danger or disaster, to safety? I have
tortured my brain with doubts and hopes in vain. You keep
your secrets well, old tree, and perhaps wisely. The future
is all my own in which to do and dare. I have courage to
pursue the open way. 'Tis from the gloomy clouds behind
I fear the bolt may come to blacken and destroy. (*Exit* R.)
    (*Enter* KATIE L. *behind trees, with a basket on her arm.*)
KATIE. Will, now, it's bothered I am intirely! My missus
axed me would I run down to the hollow wid — wid — the
basket, an' her complimints to the young ladies I'd foind
a-picknicking; and shure there's nobody picking ony thing at
all, at all. Phat will I do?
    (*Enter* GYP R. 1st *entrance with basket.*)
GYP. Bress my soul! dat ar paf jes ain't no paf at all: it's
jes de mos' circumbendus road I eber trabelled; keeps going
round and round. Fust ting I knowed, I was up to our
back-door. Had to go all ober it again. But here I is. (*Goes
up stage; meets* KATY C.)
KATY. Will, I'd loike to know — Is it there ye are, Miss
Guiney.
GYP. Miss — Miss — what dat are you say? Don't know
nuffin 'bout no such woman. Ise Gyp, I is.
KATY. Gyp, is it? Shure that's the name of a puppy.
GYP. Dat's my name, and no mistook.
KATY. Will, I never! Shure, if I had sich a name as
that, I'd go to coort, so I would. What are yees doin' here,
I'd loike to know?
GYP. Well, dat's what I call imperance. Dis am a free
country.
KATY. Fray, or not fray, I'd have yees know this counthry
belongs to my missus. Missus Rokeman an' me want no
inthruders.
GYP. Come wid de basket: somefin' to eat for de young
folks.
KATY. Did you wipe your fate, I'd loike to know?
GYP. Onto de grass — wipe — sho! go away wid yees!

Whar's de young missus? Dey must be jes rabenous.
(*Sets basket down* R.)

KATY.   Shure I've not seen them. (*Sets basket down* L.)

GYP.   Yas, wal, dey come down yere for a pickaninny.

KATY.   A what's that?

GYP.   A pickaninny, a discursion. An', miss, what you
say your name?

KATY.   Will, ye may call me Katy.

GYP.   Why, dat's de name ob de cat's baby, dat is.
Wouldn't hab dat name. You ought to go and be courted,
and hab it changed : yas, indeed!

KATY.   Oh! be aisy now : you make me blush wid shame.
Shure I've been courted by Patsy Dolan.

GYP.   Patsy Dolan : who be she?

KATY.   It's my young man, I'd have you know. Shure
he's a broth of a b'y; and it's to be married we are, one of
these days.

GYP.   Dat so? Dat's good! I sympathize wid you : yas,
indeed! Hope you'll lib out all ye days.

KATY.   Sure I'm not going to live out at all, at all : I'm
going to be married. Says Patsy to me, says he, "Katy,
your a j'wil; an' I love yees intirely, from the sole ov your
head to the crown of your feet. Will yees take me for
bether, or for worse?" Says I to Patsy, says I, "I — I
couldn't do worse, and I might do bether : so here's my
hand wid all my heart." An' that's all there is about it.
Did iver ye have a lover, Gyp?

GYP.   Did I ever? What yer take me for? Heaps an'
heaps! Why, dar was Julius Corrolanus : he — he — fought
de world ob me. Says he to me, says he, "Gyp, I lub you :
you're de idoless ob my eye, the apple-core ob my heart,
de sunflower ob my existence. All de world am sad and
dreary widout you. Can't lib widout yer, lubliest of your
sex. Come to dis year aching heart!" Says I to him, says
I, "Julius Corrolanus, dis world am full of aches and trubbles.
You're de sebenteeth man dat has told me he had a diseased
heart. · I'm not a mejum nor a phusycan, an' I don't want no
trubbles : so you can clar de kitchen jis as soon as your
aching heart will gib you bref to do it." He jes lef, he did;
and dat's all dere is about dat.

KATY.   Will, I niver! Siventeen!

GYP.   Yas : Julius Corrolanus am de sebenteeth, and dar's

anoder waiting for his chance. No use, no use! When dey talk about wedded bliss as a cure for dar aching heart, I always give um a blister: yas, indeed! Wonder whar dem ar young ladies ar.

KATY. Shure I've not seen thim.

GYP. Dis am a lonesome place, dis am. See dat ar tree dar? Dar was a tragedy done dar at de foot ob dat tree.

KATY. A trigidy! Phat's that?

GYP. Dar was a man found dead dar twenty years ago; an'—an' Miss Becky, what libs 'at our house, she was dar too.

KATY. Found dead, was she? Shure I thought she had a pale look on her!

GYP. ' No, no! ob course not. Man dead, chile alive: jes awful! Dey say dat dat ar man walks nights.

KATY (*frightened*). Yer don't mane it! A sphook, is it?

GYP. Ob course not. How could he speak if he were dead? He jes walks and groans.

KATY. Shure I'll not stay here at all, at all. It jest makes me shake to think of it. There's the basket for the young ladies, wid Mrs. Rokeman's complimints. A sphook! Oh, murther! I'd not walk here in the night if it was broad noonday! (*Exit* L.)

GYP. (*looking after her*). See her run! see her run! She's scart, she is, dat ar girl; jes as proud as — as a hen wid one chickun, wid her Datsy Polan. Can't put on no airs wid dis yer chile. Lobers am all moonshine. Wish I'd made out forty-seven stead ob eighteen; but den I was always modest, and blush easy, though I don't show it. Now to find dem ar girls. (*Exit* R.)

(*Music; then slowly enter* MEG *back* R., *past trees to* L. C. *opening; sits on bench. Music pianissimo*)

MEG. The old trysting-place again! They call me mad, and fly at my approach, and pity me. That's right, that's right: under that mask, no prying eyes can read the truth. I am free to roam and search. There was a time, what is now a disguise was a reality: I was mad. We never dreamed of that, Hector, when you and I, in the old days, sat here so lovingly together; when yonder tree concealed our little messengers of love; when we roamed these woods. and reared in fancy, love-lit castles in the future, — ah! those were happy days. And then our marriage, our pleasant voy-

age over the sea, and the vine-covered cottage beneath the
sunny skies! We were so happy then! But when my child
was born the shadow fell, and blotted out all. Eighteen years
in darkness, and then into a new life, cured of my madness,
so they said: but my husband was gone,—where, none could
tell; and· with him went our child. Oh the weary, weary
search!— here and there a ray of light, only to be quenched
in despair. (*Rises.*) But the time has come when I must
make the last desperate effort, face her, and learn the truth.
She must have had some communication from him. That
should have been the first step. But pride, as mighty as
hers, has held me back, until reason totters again. She has
made no search; has disowned me: but she must speak
(*comes down left*). I'll meet her face to face, crush back my
pride, and beg, implore, news of my lost ones. (*Exit L. first
entrance; then music stops.*)
(*Enter R. past trees to L. opening, down C., DORA and JEN-
NIE stealthily.*)

DORA. We have escaped them without notice· Now for
the note! (*Takes note from her pocket.*) I was afraid that
the interesting, love-lorn damsel would arrive before the mail
had been distributed. Now, my dainty decoy, to your hiding-
place to work mischief or fun: 'tis all the same.

JENNIE. Will she know where to find it?

DORA. Yes: I told her in my last fond epistle. (*Places
note in tree.*) What's this? The tree has done service before. See, Jennie! (*holds up a folded paper; chord.*)

JENNIE. 'Tis yellow and faded with age. What can it
mean?

(MRS. R. *appears in opening L. C. from L.*)

DORA (*examining paper*). Who knows how long it has
lain there? It must have been for years. I cannot read the
lines upon it. Ah! here's a name,— "Hector Gray."

MRS. R. (*comes forward*). "Hector Gray?"

DORA. Mrs. Rokeman!

MRS R. What have you there? Give it me, quick!
(*Snatches paper; comes L.*)

DORA I found it in the hollow trunk of this tree.

MRS. R. (*reads paper with difficulty*). "I—dying—
falls into your hands—shall be no more—my wife—Rome
—find her—I bring—her—ring. Remember—Hector
Gray." And here upon the back my name!

DORA. Can you make it out, Mrs. Rokeman?

MRS. R. (*crushing paper in her hand*). Scarcely. It's of no consequence; an old record, probably left there by one of the woodmen long years ago (*looks at it*), in the secret place where they hid their tender thoughts; and now to me — me, the slighted and wronged — he sends his dying words! Find her? No: I would not stir one step to save her. She left me for the love of an adventurer. She has no claim to my compassion. I thought he loved me; would have staked my life upon it; and, when I found they both had deceived me, my heart was turned to stone. O Hector Gray! 'twas a coward's trick by which you won your bride, and robbed me of a sister's love; so base, that, when out of the grave you call to me for help, my hardened heart repels you with hate and loathing! (*Exit* L. I E.)

JENNIE. Why, she's gone, Dora, without a word! How impolite!

DORA. That was no woodman's record.

JENNIE. There's something in that paper that affected her. How her hands shook! Oh, here's the basket! (*Goes to basket* R.)

DORA (*goes to basket* L.). And here's another!

Two baskets with a single thought,
Two meals to eat as one.

Here's Mrs. Rokeman's card on it. Ain't this jolly? Girls, girls! Scream, Jennie!

JENNIE *and* DORA. Girls, girls!

(GIRLS *flock in from* R. *through trees.*)

DORA. Here is the basket from Mrs. Delaine; and, what do you think, another bouncer from Mrs. Rokeman!

GRACE. From Mrs. Rokeman?

DORA. Yes: our high-toned and high-hilled neighbor has at last felt that touch of nature which makes the whole world kin, thanks to our Becky

(*Enter* BECKY *from* R.)

REBECCA. What has our Becky to answer for now?

DORA. A load of goodies from your would-be adopted mother, Mrs. Rokeman. (*Takes off cover.*) O My! cold chicken, sandwiches, Charlotte Russe, and, and —

REBECCA. But where's Gyp?

(*Enter* GYP. R. I-E.)

GYP. Here I is, Miss Becky! Had a heap ob trubble to fine you. Dis yere's our basket, dat oder Miss Quality brung from de big house. Speck we'd better send it back : dat's what I tink.

DORA. Send it back?' I think not. Oh, here's a lovely Washington pie !

GYP. Dat's noffin. Give dose away to de tramps down to our house.

DORA. O girls, hold me ! I shall fly ! Here's pickles ! (*holds up a bottle.*)

GIRLS (*in chorus*). Pickles !— oh !

GYP. Pickles ! dat's noffin. Bring yers a whole barrel : only couldn't roll it up de hill.

REBECCA. Come, Gyp : lay the cloth. We shall do full justice to your basket as well as Mrs. Rokeman's.

GYP. All right.

DORA. Hurry, girls ! Thanks to Mrs. Rokeman, instead of a lunch we have a banquet.

(GYP *spreads table-cloth in* C. *of stage, near* C. *tree. Music.* GIRLS *bring from each basket, and place upon cloth, food. Singing, air, "Sabre de mon Père."*)

> We spread our banquet in the forest,
>   Beneath yon proudly arching tree,
> Whose leafy branches, bending o'er us,
>   Bestows its shady canopy.
> We'll pass the time in happy converse ;
>   No care shall mar our happy day : .
> With song and jest and merry laughter
>   The hours too quickly pass away.
> Haste to the banquet, the banquet, the banquet,
>   Haste to the banquet, the banquet we have spread ;
> Haste to the banquet, the banquet, the banquet,
>   Haste to the banquet, the banquet we have spread !

(*At the conclusion of song, all seat themselves about* ad libitum *and eat.* GYP *passes plate to* REBECCA ; *then stands* L. C. *opening; or assisting as need be.*)

DORA (R.). Now, isn't this jolly ? And yet Jennie is satisfied with a musical feast. Music the food of love !— nonsense !

JENNIE (L.). Oh ' you may laugh ; but I contend there is enough in music to furnish a feast, and I can prove it.

DORA. I should like to see the proof. — Have some cold chicken, Becky ?

REBECCA. No, I thank you.

DORA. In the first place, where will you find a table?

JENNIE. I should go to the piano for that, and take the key-board.

DORA. And the piano-cover for a table-cloth. Now set your table.

JENNIE. Well, for plates, I should go to the musical scale and take flats.

DORA. Mercy! Why don't you take whole notes? they are round, and not apt to crack. What for knives?

JENNIE. Sharps, of course; and forks, the tuning-fork, of course; and for spoons —

DORA. As it is a lovers' feast, they won't want any besides themselves. But you need a caster.

JENNIE. There are four on the piano.

DORA. Gracious! — what a head! What next?

JENNIE. That will do for the table. Now we want bread: the staff will do for that.

DORA. I see; bread being the staff of life.

GRACE. Why not go to the drum? You could always get fresh rolls from that. (*All laugh.*)

DORA. Grace, have a sandwich? you must be faint. — Come, Jennie: we want four courses, — soup, fish, meats, and dessert. Where will you go for your soups?

JENNIE. They're in every opera.

SADIE. Make it yourself. You can always find a bone, — a trombone. (*All laugh.*)

DORA. Lucky thought! 'Tis an ill wind that blows nobody any good. Next, fish.

JENNIE. You can always find a perch on the piano-stool.

SADIE. Or in a net, — the clarinet.

GYP. Yas, indeed; or in a horn, — the fish-horn. (*All laugh.*)

DORA. That's enough. Pass on to the next. Come, meats.

JENNIE. " Meet me by moonlight alone : " how's that?

ALL. Horrid!

GYP. Git it ob de drum. Dar's allays good mutton under de sheep-skin : dat's so (*laughs*).

JENNIE. Then, for birds —

DORA. There's always a brace on the musical scale.

GYP. What kind ob birds be dose, Miss Dora?

DORA. The do-do's, of course (*laugh*). Then, for vege-
tables, we always have beats. Now for dessert.

JENNIE. Apples, pears, oranges —

DORA. Nonsense! There's nothing musical about those.

JENNIE. Yes, indeed! — their peel.

DORA. Oh! goodness! horrible! Quite enough! The
feast of love indeed! (*All laugh.*)

(*Enter from R., past trees to L. C. opening,* CLARISSA.)

CLARISSA. Sublime spectacle of rural simplicity!

DORA. How d'ye do, Miss Codman! "Won't you come
and take tea in the arbor?"

REBECCA (*rises*). Glad to see you. (*All rise.* GYP *clears
stage and packs baskets during the scene.*) Will you taste
our homely fare?

CLARISSA. Thank you. None for me (*sighs*). I have
no appetite. I am wasting away beneath the devastating
passion which has taken possession of my tender heart.
Love, girls, — love is a jealous master: it permits no rival
to approach its throne. It hath no kindred with eating and
drinking, and that sort of thing.

DORA. Thank Goodness, I'm not in love.

CLARISSA. Ah, child! your time will come, when the
flutter of a first love will agitate your youthful breast; when
love-lit visions will hover about your pillow as they have come
to me. (*Comes down* R.) O Theophilus! my Theophilus!
your invisible presence is my joy by day, my guardian angel
by night. Where'er I walk — (*Walks across stage.*)

GYP. Please step off de tablecloth, Miss Codman! Dat
ain't a carpet.

CLARISSA. I beg pardon. I was so rapt —

GYP. Why, who — who — rapped yer? I nebber struck
yer.

CLARISSA (*goes up towards tree* R.). (*Aside.*) I must seek
the hollow tree, within whose confines rest what I hold so
dear.

DORA (*to* JENNIE, L.). She's after the note! (*Aloud.*)
Going, Miss Codman?

CLARISSA (*turns*). Oh, no! I propose to meander in this
lovely retreat, so eloquent of love and Arcadian quiet.

DORA. O Becky! — here a moment. (REBECCA *comes
down* L.). I forgot to tell you, when I placed the note for
Miss Codman in that tree, I found an old yellow paper, that
must have been there for years.

REBECCA. You found it? Oh, give it to me quick!

DORA. I haven't it. Just as I had made out the name signed to it, — Hector Gray, — Mrs. Rokeman snatched it from my hand.

REBECCA. Mrs. Rokeman?

DORA. Yes. She read it, and seemed much moved by its contents. — Why, Becky, what's the matter? How pale you look!

REBECCA. Dora, I was found at the foot of that tree!

DORA. You! Then perhaps that paper concerned you.

REBECCA. I'm sure it did. O Dora! I have both longed for and dreaded the disclosure that paper must bring. I have foolishly suffered, because I know nothing of my former life; but, now the knowledge is so near, I tremble with fear, lest the disclosure which must come may be fraught with shame! (*Covers her face with her hands.*)

DORA. Nonsense! Are you not one of us? You have done no wrong. What shame can come to you? Your own true heart has made you loving and beloved, and you will always be our own dear Becky. (*Puts her arm about her, leads her up* C.; *girls gather around them.* CLARISSA *comes down with note; holds it up.*)

CLARISSA. My tiny messenger of love! (*Opens and reads.*) "Dearest, sweetest, and loveliest!" (*Kisses note.*) Truthful Theophilus! (*Reads.*) "I pine for thee as I wander around these mournful pines, a sapless!" Oh, no! "a hapless wretch! I must see you. My eyes, even now, as you read, are upon you. When all is still, when you are alone, I will appear. Faint not, dearest; nerve yourself for the shock; and believe me ever your own true, devoted Theophilus." Oh, I shall see him in all his native majesty! Oh happiness of joy unspeakable! (*Turns quickly.*) Come, girls: isn't it time you were going home? It's getting late, and these woods are awful lonesome after dark.

REBECCA. We were just thinking of moving. Will you accompany us?

CLARISSA. Not just yet: this quiet solitude is very inviting to my reflective moods. I will tarry a while, and refresh myself.

GYP (*with baskets on her arm, crosses to* R., *first* E.). De refreshments jes moving: can't tarry no longer. Ef you get

hungry, come down to the house and recooper up yerself.
(*Exit first*, E. R.)

REBECCA. Come, girls. (GIRLS *pass behind trees in
couples.*) Good-by, Miss Codman! (*Puts arm about* DORA.)
We have had a pleasant day, — perhaps the last happy day I
shall spend in this spot. (*Exit slowly with* DORA *after the
other girls pass tree to* R.)

CLARISSA. They are gone! How my heart flutters! I
shall meet him, — meet him by moonlight alone! And
there's no moon : what a shame! I wonder if my back-hair
is all right. (*Arranges curls.*) Lucky I curled my hair
this morning, though I did scorch it with the hot iron!
He's coming! Theophilus, my loved one, is coming! Wonder if my dress hangs right behind. I must look pale; get
the color out of my face. (*Takes handkerchief out of her
pocket, and rubs cheeks violently.*) Theophilus! — my Theophilus!

Song. — Air, "Baby Mine."

I am waiting here for thee,
Lover mine, lover mine, –
Here beside the old oak-tree,
Lover mine.
Oh, with what a glad surprise
I shall look into thine eyes,
Where all my kingdom lies,
Lover mine, lover mine;
Where all my kingdom lies,
Lover mine!

How shall I receive him? A pensive attitude will be most
becoming. (*Places left hand under right elbow, finger of
right hand on lip, eyes rolled up.*) Ha! I hear his step!
Be still, little fluttering heart!

(DORA *appears from* R. *wrapped in a long cloak with a
slouched hat concealing her face; she steps between trees.*)

DORA (*imitating deep voice*). "Where art thou now, my
beloved?"

CLARISSA (*with a slight scream turns*). Ah, 'tis he! 'tis
he! — so like the face of my dreams! The commanding fig-
ure! Strange man, individual in disguise, who art thou?
Dost thou come to affront a simple country maiden? or art
thou, say, art thou —

DORA. "Clarissa!"

CLARISSA. 'Tis he!—that voice, so tender and loving! I come to thee, my beloved. But tell me that I mistake thee not. You are? (*Goes up to her with extended arms.*)

DORA. "Yes, Clarissa, I am (*throws off cloak and hat*) Theophilus Montague!"

(*Girls flock in back* R.)

CLARISSA. Oh, deceived, deceived!—lost! (*Falls upon rustic bench* L.)

(DORA *and girls laughing as curtain descends.*)

END SECOND ACT.

ACT III.

SCENE. — *Parlor in* MRS. ROKEMAN'S *house. Open doors*
C., *backed by garden; windows* R. *and* L. *of doors* C., *with*
curtains; small table at window R., *vase of flowers on it;*
chair near; small table at window L., *with dish of fruit*
on it and plates; upright piano against side L., *at which*
SADIE *is seated; door* L., *between piano and flat; door*
opposite R.; *arm-chair* L. C., *in which* MRS. ROKEMAN *is*
seated; ottoman R. C., *on which* JENNIE *and* MELLIE *are*
seated, with an open book of engravings; EMMA *stands*
behind, looking over. Arm-chair R., *in which* GRACE *is*
seated; MARIA on hassock, at her left; ALICE *stands at*
her right, leaning against chair; GUSSIE *stands* L., *be-*
tween piano and MRS. R. *Before the curtain rises,* SADIE,
or any other member of the company who may be selected
as pianist, commences a solo, concluding it after the cur-
tain has been raised. Then introduce such vocal and in-
strumental specialties as may be desired, concluding with

(*Chorus. Air,* "*Believe me if all those endearing young*
charms.")

> Remember, while life's fond, enchanting young days
>   Are so bright with the blossoms of joy,
> There are sad hearts to lighten, and weak souls to raise,
>   And wrongs to forgive and destroy.
> For the heart that is truly blest never dismays
>   At the task which stern duty may give:
> With its balm for all ills in life's devious ways,
>   Remember to forget and forgive.

DORA.   There, Mrs. Rokeman, I believe we have ex-
hausted our repertoire; and the girls are just dying to have
a ramble in your beautiful garden. Aren't you, girls?

GIRLS (*in chorus*). Oh, yes!

MRS. R. Pardon me! You have entertained me so charmingly, I quite forgot my duties as hostess. But — your friend? She does not come.

DORA. Oh! Becky will come, never fear. She is very particular to leave all neat and tidy at home. We might meet her, if you would let us go into the garden.

JENNIE (*twitching* DORA'S *dress*). Why, Do! How impolite!

DORA. Can't help it. I must have a run in that garden.

MRS. R. (*rising: all rise*). You are free to roam where'er you please. My house, my grounds, all are at your pleasure. My garden has been so long silently beautiful, I am anxious to hear it ring with the music of your merry voices.

GIRLS (*in chorus*). Oh, thank you! Thank you!

DORA. Come on, girls! They laugh the heartiest who run the fastest. Catch me if you can! (*Darts out* C. *door, and off* L., *followed by the* GIRLS, *laughing*.)

MRS. R. Remember. Yes, that word pierced my heart with a pain so sharp and sudden, that I almost cried out. Have I done right? I have rent away the gloomy veil that for twenty years has enveloped this house, and let in the sunlight of youthful faces and the music of glad voices. With my own hands I have brought back the sweet happy days of girlhood. For what? To mock me with one gleam of the paradise of peace, only to make still darker the gloomy future. [*Exit door* L.

(*Enter from* R., *through door* C., REBECCA *and* MRS. DELAINE.)

REBECCA. Come along, Mother Chirrup. You can't run away from me!

MRS. D. Bless my soul! I never expected to enter these doors again. Nobody wants an old woman like me. I tell you, Becky, I'm going straight home. There's the bread to make and the cow to milk —

REBECCA. No. Mother Chirrup. Here you are. and here you stay. It's my company, and I've liberty to invite whom I please. Take off your bonnet. Mother Chirrup.

MRS. D. I shall do no such thing.

REBECCA. Very well. Then I shall do it for you. (*Removes bonnet*.) I've invited Clarissa Codman : and, when she comes. you two can have a grand time talking over your old love-affairs.

MRS. D. Me? I never had such a thing in my life.

REBECCA. Remember, you are to find out the contents
of that mysterious paper found in the woods yesterday.

MRS. D. Oh! I thought you didn't bring me here' just
for company.

REBECCA. Why, you wicked old lady! I've a great mind
to shake you. Sit down, and be sociable. (*Pushes her into
chair* R.)

MRS. D. Sociable here? Why, Becky, it just makes me
shiver to be in this house.

REBECCA (*placing shawl and bonnet on chair near* R. *window*). Then we will have a fire built for your special accom-
modation.

(*Enter* MRS. R. *door* L.)

MRS. R. I'm glad to see you. (*Gives hand to* REBECCA.)

REBECCA. Thank you, Mrs. Rokeman.   •

MRS. R. And my old friend Mary. Welcome! (*Gives
hand to* MRS. D.)

MRS. D. I didn't mean to come, Mrs. Helen; but she
would make me. She's a tyrant, that she is. She makes
me do just as she pleases.

REBECCA. Don't scold, Mother Chirrup; for, when you
scold, your head shakes; and, when your head shakes, your
cap always gets awry.

MRS. D. (*puts hand to cap*). Mercy on me!

REBECCA. I am a little late, Mrs. Rokeman. Would you
believe it? I forgot the particularly-invited guest, — the
cake. And, after setting out, I was obliged to return and
give Gyp directions about bringing it. Are the girls here?
(GIRLS *laugh outside*.) Oh, yes! I hear them. May I join
them?

MRS. R. Certainly.

REBECCA. Then I will leave Mother Chirrup with you.
Don't let her scold, Mrs. Rokeman; for she has taken great
pains with her cap, and, should it come to pieces, great would
be the fall thereof.   [*Exit* C. *and off* L.

MRS. R. (*sits chair* L. C.) Mary.

MRS. D. (*jumps up*). Yes, marm. (*Aside.*) Dear me! I
thought I was in service again. (*Sits and straightens up
very prim.*) Well, Mrs. Rokeman.

MRS. R. 'Tis many years since you left this house,
Mary.

MRS. D. Twenty years this June. The day after your sister was married.

MRS. R. We will not speak of my sister.

MRS. D. (*rises*). Indeed, then I wish you a very good-afternoon. (*Moves towards door* C. MRS. R. *rises, and stops her.*)

MRS. R. Stop, Mary, we must not part again in anger. You may speak of whom you please. Be seated.

MRS. D. (*sits*). Well, if I may speak, I've got nothing more to say.

MRS. R. Your presence here, Mary, recalls many pleasing recollections of the time when my father was alive. This was a merry place then.

MRS. D. Indeed it was. The squire, your father, was a gentle man, free-handed and warm-hearted; your sister Clara as merry and bright as a fairy. (*Sighs.*) Dear, dear! what could have become of her?

MRS. R. Your adopted daughter Rebecca interests me very much. Where did you find her? ·

MRS. D. (*aside*). Becky — she wants her; but she can't have her. (*Aloud.*) Oh! she's a poorhouse child.

MRS. R. And her father and mother?

MRS. D. Dead, poor thing, dead. Did you never hear any thing of Clara?

MRS. R. Never. How old is Rebecca?

MRS. D. About the age of your sister Clara when she married. (*Aside.*) She can't choke me off.

MRS. R. Eighteen?

MRS. D. Exactly. (*Aside.*) How well she remembers! (*Aloud.*) Why don't you make some inquiries for Clara?

MRS. R. I know no way, even had I the desire.

MRS. D. (*aside*). Still hard and revengeful. (*Aloud.*) No way? Then I'd find one. She must have gone somewhere, and the world is not so big but what a warm heart and a long purse might be able to find trace of her.

MRS. R. Possibly. Shall we join the young ladies?

MRS. D. By and by. They do not need us, and possibly we might interfere with their pleasure as you did yesterday.

MRS. R. I!

MRS. D. Yes: one of them found an old paper hid in the hollow oak. You came upon them suddenly, and snatched

it away before they had gratified a natural curiosity to learn
its contents.

MRS. R.   It would not have interested them.

MRS. D.   But it did you.

MRS. R.   Me!

MRS. D.   Yes; for, while you read it, your face paled and
your hands shook.

MRS. R. (*with an effort*).   It was an almost unintelligible
scrawl from the hand of a dying man, Hector Gray.

MRS. D.   Hector Gray?   Mercy!   Clara's husband.
What did it say?

MRS. R. (*takes paper from her pocket*).   You may read it.
(*Hands paper.*)

MRS. D.   Let me get my glasses. (*Puts on glasses.*) It's
very old and yellow with age. (*Reads slowly.*) ".Dying.—
wife—Rome." I can make nothing of it. Yes, yes, I can:
Clara was in Rome, and he—

MRS. R.   Was on his way to me, to me. Tired of her,
he turned to me, no doubt to confess his error, and implore
pardon.

MRS. D.   Your own love deceived you. 'Twas Clara he
loved, and her alone.

MRS. R.   His last words were for me.

MRS. D.   That you might seek your sister. There could
be no other motive, save one.

MRS. R.   And that?

MRS. D.   To place— (*Aside.*) I see it all: I must lose my
Becky, but not until justice is done to Clara. (*Aloud.*) You
will seek her in Rome? You will go to her?

MRS. R.   No.

MRS. D.   Then I will. (*Rises.*) I'm an old woman,
hardly fitted for a task that requires strength and endurance;
but I would cross seas, mountains, to clasp in my arms once
more the child who nestled there long, long ago. Helen
Rokeman, you are proud of your name, and yet you would
let the darling of your house wander among strangers.
Thank Heaven, I have no such pride to check the promptings
of my heart. I will find her if she be living.

MRS. R.   Shall we join the young ladies?

MRS. D. (*returns paper*).   When you please. I want
Becky.

MRS. R. (*goes to door* C).   Then follow me. (*Turns.*)

Mary, if I seem cold and cruel, remember that all the brightness was blotted from my life by the man who made my sister happy and me miserable. Come. [*Exit* L.

MRS. D. Ah! the Delmar pride is stubborn. But if you knew all — if you knew as I do now who will inherit this grand estate, your pride would be humbled, my lady. (*Exit* C. *to* L. MEG *creeps on from door* R., *and watches them off.*)

MEG. Too late. By the old familiar way I have crept into her house, only to miss the opportunity of meeting her alone. (GIRLS *laugh outside.*) Merry voices and gay company (*looks off*), bright and happy faces about her. She greets them with smiles. What masquerade is here! They told me she was cold and haughty, held herself aloof from her neighbors. Have I been mistaken? Is there warm life within that marble statue, feeling within that obdurate heart? If it be so, my wrongs will find a way to reach it, my despair the power to touch it. [*Exit door* L.

(*Enter, door* R., KATY, *with a letter in her hand.*)

KATY (*turning letter over and over*). An' sure I got a love-lether frum Patsy; an' phat will I do wid it I dunno. I can't rade, and the misthress is away wid the company girls. How will I find out phat's inside it? It's bothered I am intirely.

(*Enter from* L., *through* C. *door,* DORA.)

DORA. Ah, Katy! Is it ther yees are? Where's Mrs. Delaine's shawl? I see it. (*Goes towards window* R.)

KATY. If yees plase, Miss Dora, might I be afther troubling yees?

DORA (*comes down*). Certainly, Katy. What's the trouble?

KATY. If yees plase, I have a lether.

DORA. From the ould counthry?

KATY. No, indade: it's from — it's from — sure you'll be afther laughin' if I tole yees.

DORA. Then you needn't tell me, Katy: I can guess. It's a love-letter.

KATY. An' who towld yees that?

DORA. Yourself, Katy, by the blushes on your cheeks and the sparkle in your eyes. You want me to read it for you?

KATY. If yees plase, Miss Dora. (*Hands letter.*)

DORA (*opening letter*). I shall learn all your secrets, Katy. Perhaps the young man would not like that.

KATY. Thin yees moight shkip the sacrets.

DORA (*laughs*). All right. Katy. (*Reads.*) " Lovely Katy."

KATY. That's me. Sure that's no sacret.

DORA (*reads*). " I take me pin in hand wid a bating heart, to till yees uv the sthrong wakeniss I have for yees."

KATY. Yees moight shkip that.

DORA (*reads*). " I have nather ate, dhrunk, nor slipt, for a wake."

KATY. Will, that jist accounts for the wakeniss.

DORA (*reads*). " Barrin' my thray males a day, an' me pipe an' tobacyer."

KATY. An' he wid the hearty appetite !

DORA (*reads*). An' all me slapeliss nights are fill wid drames of yees, Katy Mavourneen."

KATY. Sure he's the darlin'.

DORA (*reads*). " I have yees phortygraff nailed to the hid uv me bid ; and ivery night, afther I've blown out the candle wid me fingers, I tak a good look at it, an', if ye'll belave me, there's not a dry thread in me eyes."

KATY. Sure he was alwus tinder-hearted.

DORA (*reads*). " If yees don't belave me, tak a good look at yees own face before yees open the leather, and see if I have not cause to wape."

KATY. Sure I ought to have known that before the lether came.

DORA (*reads*). " If yees foind these tinder loins blotted wid tears, it's all owing to the bad quality uv the ink, which has compilled me to pin this wid a pincil."

KATY. That's no mather.

DORA (*reads*). " If yees don't recave this lether, or can't rade it, niver moind : ye'll know that all that's in it is the truth, an' nades nather radin' or writin' to till the same. So name the day, Katy darlin', whin me single blissidniss is to exphire, an' the mathrimoonial noose shlipped over the hid of yees lovin' and consolin'

PATSY DOLAN.

" P.S. — These last lines are the poethry uv love.

" SECOND P.S. — To be rid fhirst. I inclose a ring for yees finger, which same yees will find in me nixt lether." That's all, Katy. (*Hands back letter.*)

KATY. It's jist illigent. I'm obleeged to yees.

DORA (*takes shawl from chair*). Quite welcome, Katy.

When you get ready to name the day. I'll answer it for you. But be quick, Katy; for the poor fellow will not live long on "only his thray males a day, an' his pipe an' tobacyer." (*Runs off* C. *to* L.)

KATY (*looks at letter*). Sure it's a darlin' lether, an' Patsy Dolan's a broth uv a bye.

(*Enter from* R., *through* C. *door*, GYP, *with basket of cake covered with a napkin.*)

GYP. Ah, dar you is, Katy! Whar's de misses? Whar's Miss Becky? Whar's eberybody?

KATY. In the garden, sure. Yees may coom in, if yees wipe yers fate.

GYP. Yas, indeed! How yer was? ,And how's Patsy Dolan?

KATY. He's will. I've jist recaved a lether from him.

GYP. Dat so? Dat's good! Lub-letters am bery consolin' to de flutterin' heart. Here's de cake for Miss Becky. (*Sets it on top of piano.*) Got a letter, hab you? S'pose you red it frough and frough.

KATY. Sure I can't rade at all, at all.

GYP. Dat so? Well, well! De ignoramance ob de foreign poperlation am distressin'.

KATY. Can you rade?

GYP. Read? What you take me for? How else could I debour de heaps and heaps ob lub-letters dat I constantly receibe from my adorers? ·

KATY (*aside*). Faith, I'd loike to hear Patsy's lether again. (*Aloud.*) Thin plase rade this for me. (*Hands letter.*)

GYP (*confused*). Wh-wh-what you take me fur? (*Aside.*) Golly! she cotch me dèn. (*Aloud.*) No. chile: dose tender confections am fur you alone, and dey shouldn't be composed to de world.

KATY. An' sure yees can't rade.

GYP. What's that? Can't read? (*Takes letter, and turns it round several times.*) Berry long letter. Want to hear it all?

KATY. Ivery word.

GYP (*aside*). Mussn't gib in. Spec dase all alike. (*Aloud.*) Ob course, ob course. (*Pretends to read.*) "Lubliest ob your sexes."

KATY. Sure that's not there.

GYP (*shows letter*). See fur yerself, see fur yerself.

KATY. Go on wid the lether.

GYP. "Sublimest ob de fair sexes, dis am a whale ob tears. Dar ain't no sunshine of moonshine widout you."

KATY. That's not thrue at all, at all.

GYP (*shows letter*). Read it yerself, read yerself.

KATY. Go on wid the lether.

GYP. "De moon on de lake am beamin', de lubly sunflower perfumeries in de garden, de tuneful frogs meliferously warble in de riber, an' de breezes blow fro' de treeses; but my lub, my lub, whar, oh, whar am she?"

KATY. I don't belave —

GYP (*as before*). See fur yerself; see fur yerself!

KATY. Oh, quit yees talkin' an' talkin'. Go on wid the lether.

GYP.

> "My lub she isn't hansum,
> My lub she isn't fair;
> But to cook de beef and 'taters
> Can't beat her anywhar."

Dat's potry, Katy, dat is; alwus find lots ob dat in lub-letters: it gibs dem a flabor.

KATY. I don't belave it's there.

GYP (*as before*). See fur yerself; see fur yerself!

KATY. Go on wid the lether.

GYP. Luf me see wha was I. "Come rest on dis yere head your aching breast." Dey all got dat, Katy, an' — an' (*aside*), well, I'se jest puzzled fur more : guess we'll hab some more potry (*aloud*) an' — an', —

> "We'll dance all night 'till broad daylight,
> An' go home wid de girls in de morning."

KATY. It's no such thing! Yer desavin' me, so yees are Me Patsy wouldn't go home wid the girls at all, at all.

GYP. See fur yerself; see fur yerself!

KATY (*snatching letter*). So I will. It's false and desateful yees are, for Miss Dora rid the lether, an' — an' — it was jist illegant so it was ; an' it's yersilf, — bad luck to the loikes ov yees, whin yees can't rade! an' it's the blissid troth I'm tillin', — invintin' a bit uv blarney to make trouble betwane a poor girl an' her Patsy. Away wid yees!

[*Exit door* R.

GYP. Well, I guess she fooled me dat time. No use.

Dar's alwus trubble interferin' in lub affairs, jest like domestic affairs: when man and wife am fighting, ef you try to be a messenger ob peace, ef you don't look out, you'll git de broomstick onto yer own head.

(*Enter door* C. MRS. R. *and* REBECCA.)

REBECCA. Dear Mrs. Rokeman, it is very kind of you to give us this charming afternoon.

MRS. R. My dear girl, I am indebted to you for a very great pleasure. I have been very cold and unsocial in shutting myself away from the lovely and lively society which you can summon about you with a smile, and whom you seem born to command.

REBECCA. I'm glad you like them. Oh, here's Gyp!— Did you bring the cake?

GYP. Yas, Miss Becky, dar it am on de organ.

REBECCA. Thank you; you may go to Mother Chirrup for further orders.

GYP. Yas, Miss Becky.   [*Exit door* C. *off* L.

REBECCA (*takes basket*). Now, Mrs. Rokeman, you shall be the first to judge our new experiment. Luckily we are alone: the girls would be so mortified if it should happen to be a failure.

MRS. R. (*sits arm-chair* L. C.). Never fear; I shall be a lenient judge.

REBECCA. Oh, you must tell the truth! (*Takes plate from window* L., *and places it in* MRS. R.'S *lap.*) It looks nice, doesn't it?

MRS. R. Very tempting. Shall I try it?

REBECCA (*presenting basket*). If you please. (MRS. R. *raises a slice.*) Not that please. Try this (*points*), there's an almond sticking out. Don't you like almonds?

MRS. R. Very much. (*Takes slice of cake, and lays it on her plate.*)

REBECCA (*carries basket back to piano*). Our fate is in your hands.

MRS. R. (*takes cake in her hands, holding it above plate*). Thank you. (*Breaks it. Ring falls jingling into plate.*) What's this?

REBECCA (*turns quickly*). My ring! Found at last! Who would ever have dreamed of finding it there! It must have slipped off while I was mixing the cake.

MRS. R. (*who has taken up the ring, and is examining it,*

with much emotion). Your ring? Yours? How came you by this ring? Speak, girl!

REBECCA (*kneels beside* MRS. R. *without turning back to audience*). It was hanging about my neck when I was found.

MRS. R. Found where?

REBECCA. In the woods, near the great elm, eighteen years ago.

MRS. R. Eighteen years ago?

REBECCA. Yes, in the arms of a dead man. No one knew his story; no clew to his former history could be found. Why, Mrs. Rokeman, how pale you are! Are you ill?

MRS. R. (*with an effort*). 'Tis nothing. This ring — it has a motto.

REBECCA. "Remember." Yes, a mocking motto. It bids me do what I have no power to perform, — to remember something which I have never known; something in the past for which I grope in vain amid the darkness. O Mrs. Rokeman! you are rich and powerful; help me to find some trace of her who gave me birth, my mother, and I will bless you. (*Bows her head in her hands.*)

MRS. R. (*places hand on her head*). Poor child, poor child! You are right. I am rich and powerful, and I will help you; and, should I succeed, your blessing would be the greastest reward I could desire. Will you trust your ring to me, Rebecca?

REBECCA (*rising*). Willingly. (*Takes plate to table.*)

MRS. R. (*rising*). And, if I succeed, you will pardon me?

REBECCA. Pardon? You never wronged me, and now you will be my champion. (*Takes her hand.*) Heaven bless you! Come failure or success, I shall love you with my whole heart. (*Kisses hand.*)

MRS. R. (*aside*). Heaven make me worthy of that love. (*Aloud.*) Go to your friends, my child, and fear not: your interests I shall (*looks at ring*) "remember."

REBECCA. A thousand, thousand thanks! How glad the girls will be to know I have found my ring! (*Runs off door* C. *to* L.)

MRS. R. There's no escape. I must set myself to the task too long neglected. I thought myself wronged because one I loved turned from me to one who had all his heart after my promise (*looks at ring*), "Remember, his choice shall be sacred; it shall never break our love." And I turned traitor, shut my heart against her, and cursed them both in my bitterness and despair. And now this child, her image, pleads to me for help. Twenty years of sinful hate swept away by the pleadings of a girl. I must repair the wrong. All else failing, I must, I will, win her love. (*Comes down* R., *looking at ring.*)

(*Enter* MEG, *door* L.)

MEG. Alone at last.

MRS. R. (*turns*). You here?

MEG. Yes, I, — Meg, crazy Meg. Ha, ha! not a welcome visitor to your grand house. The lady of the hill. Ha, ha! rich and mighty, but so proud and haughty she dwells alone, and hears not the cry of want or pity; for, from her heart there wells a bitter cry to drown all else, — " Remorse, remorse."

MRS. R. Woman, begone! I know you not.

MEG. You do (*solemnly*): "remember."

MRS. R. " Remember!" Who are you?

MEG (*throws off gray wig*). Tell me, you.

MRS. R. My sister Clara! Oh, welcome, welcome! (*Goes towards her with open arms.*)

MEG (*waves her back*). Back, we are strangers.

MRS. R. Strangers? O Clara! sister!

MEG. Peace! We are no longer sisters. "Remember, his choice shall be sacred: it shall never break our love." I have kept the compact, have you? Mid misery and want, when the clouds were thick about me. and when he I loved forsook me, I waited, longed, for a loving word from over the sea. It never came.

MRS. R. Clara, you have been wronged, cruelly wronged. I was pitiless, relentless: but now all is changed. This very day, within an hour, I have heard that which, but for your coming, would have set me on the road for Rome to-morrow. (*Kneels.*) O Clara, sister, on my knees I implore your pardon and forgiveness! Be reconciled; I am ready to share all with you.

MEG. Too late. I have lost my husband and my child; your love I lost years ago; there is nothing worth living for now. Here amid the scenes of my happy youth I should go mad.

MRS. R. (*rises*). You will not take my hand?

MEG. No. (*Turns away.*)

MRS. R. You are right. For the wrong I have commit-
ted I must make atonement, and I will.

MEG. How? Can you give me back my husband?

MRS. R. No, Clara, I cannot do that. But I can give you
convincing proof of his love and devotion to you. He did
not desert you. He died in the loving duty of bearing his
child from your arms to mine.

(REBECCA *appears from* L., *stops in door-way* C.)

MEG. Dead! My husband? How learned you this?

MRS. R. From this (*showing paper*), found yesterday in
an old tree on my — our estate.

MEG (*snatches paper*). 'Tis his writing. O Hector,
Hector, my husband! Go on, go on.

MRS. R. (*shows ring*). Here is a ring perhaps you will
recognize.

MEG. Your ring?

MRS. R. No, mine has never left my finger (*holds up finger*) as you may see : this is yours.

MEG. My ring, mine? How came you by that? If you
have any mercy, speak.

MRS. R. I might say more to my sister, but not to a
stranger.

MEG (*falls on her knees*). O Helen, sister! have mercy.
Speak, speak!

MRS. R. (*raises her*). Be patient and listen. Eighteen
years ago your husband, Hector Gray, was found dead in
the woods, with a child fast locked in his arms.

MEG. Living or dead — the child?

MRS. R. Living.

MEG. Thank Heaven!

MRS. R. Around its neck was fastened this ring.

MEG. And the child?

MRS. R. Was taken by a good woman, and brought up as
her own. To-day that ring fell into my hands, and for the
first time (believe me, Clara) I became aware of that child's
parentage.

MEG (*comes to* L.) My child lives — my child! Oh, bless
you, Helen! sister, where is she?

REBECCA. Here, mother, here. (*Runs into* MEG'S *arms.*
GIRLS *all appears behind.*)

MRS. R. She speaks the truth, Clara.

MEG. My daughter, my dear, dear daughter!

REBECCA. O mother! I have so longed for this moment, My dear, dear mother!

MRS. R. Clara, am I forgiven? (MEG *throws herself into her arms; they embrace; then* MRS. R. *holds out her arms to* REBECCA, *and they embrace; then the three stand* L. C. *conversing.*)

MRS. D. (*outside*). Where's Becky? (*Enter* C., REBECCA *passes to* R.) Come, child, we must go home at once. To-morrow I must set out on a long journey to find (*sees* MEG) to find — no, no, she's found, she's found. Clara, Clara! (MEG *runs into her arms.*) Home, home at last.

MEG. Yes, dear old nurse, to the happy home of my childhood (*turns and takes* MRS. R.'s *hand*), to the loving heart of my sister.

MRS. R. Yes, Mary, the adamantine walls have given way.
(REBECCA *goes up* C.)

MRS. D. Ah! I knew it would all come right at last. It's glorious; but there's something better to come; something that will amaze you (*with a very important air*); something known only to me, — my Becky —

REBECCA (*coming between* MRS. D. *and* MEG *from behind, puts her arms about their waists*) — has two mothers now.
(DORA *and* JENNIE *come down* R.)

MRS. D. Oh, you've found it out!

DORA. Of course she has: the undoing of the mystery was Becky's doing, you may be sure of that.

REBECCA. No it was our cake.

DORA. It's all the same: I knew you had a hand in it.

REBECCA. And a ring.
(*Enter* CLARISSA *door* C. *from* R.)

CLARISSA. Girls, dear girls, give me joy! (*Comes down to* L. *corner.*) Good-afternoon, Mrs. Rokeman: I couldn't come sooner for I had a caller, a dear, delightful caller. And who do you think it was?

DORA. Theophilus Montague?

CLARISSA. You saucy, saucy thing! It was Deacon Sapham, that dear, good, noble, delightful man. Give me joy: he has asked me to share his future, to become the partner of his joys. The d —

DORA. Deacon Sapham! A widower with nine children! O Miss Codman! how could you?

CLARISSA.   I shall love them all.   I shall call my little chickens under my wing and be so happy!

MRS. D.   Mercy sakes, Clarissa, don't be a fool! (*Crosses over to her.*) You're not the first woman who's been through the woods, and taken up a crooked stick at last.

CLARISSA.   He is my first, my only love.

DORA.   Except Theophilus Montague.

CLARISSA.   Oh, you little wretch!

(*Enter* R. *door* KATY.)

KATY.   The table's riddy, Mrs. Rokeman.   (*Comes down* R. *to* DORA.) The nixt lether have coome, and the ring also.

DORA (*to* KATY). Sure he's a broth uv a bye, Patsy Dolan. (MRS. ROKEMAN R. C., MEG L. C., REBECCA C.   *Enter door* C., GYP; *comes down to piano* L.)

MEG (*to* REBECCA). Am I not a happy mother, after the years of misery and estrangement, to find my child at last all a mother's heart could wish!

REBECCA.   I have so hungered for that love so long denied me that this joyful re-union seems almost a dream.   O mother! happy days are before us.

MRS. R.   Before us all, I trust.   My sister takes her place once more among us to share with me the fortune our father left; but the reigning mistress of this home will be the child who has united us.

MRS. D.   That's my Becky!

DORA.   Our Becky.

MRS. R.   The table waits.   Come let us be merry.

GYP (*takes cake-basket from piano*). Don't forget de cake.

DORA.   No, indeed!   "Rebecca's Triumph" must crown the festive board.   For if the cooking-club had not made that cake, and if Becky hadn't lost her ring in it, and if —

JENNIE.   If you don't stop talking, we shall never get to the table.

DORA.   I'm dumb.

REBECCA.   And so am I, Dora, with wonder, to think that I, the waif of the woods, should stand among you with the dark mystery all cleared away, and a new life opening before me full of hope and promise.   If, in my new station, the old loves and friendships be still mine, this will be a day to remember (*taking* MRS. R.'s *hand, puts arm about* MEG'S *waist*). There's no love like mother-love, no tie so sacred as that of kindred. These are mine, and over doubts and fears I triumph at last.

MRS. D. As I knew you would; as you deserve.

DORA. So say we all of us. The cooking club is proud of its member, and will never forget the day it had a helping hand in — in — what was it, girls?

GIRLS (*in chorus*). " Rebecca's Triumph."

(Music and curtain.)

Electrotyped and printed by Rand, Avery, & Co., Boston.

No.1 Reading Club and Handy Speaker.

Edited by GEORGE M. BAKER.

Price, cloth, 50 cents; paper, 15 cents.

CONTENTS.

No man is better qualified to edit this series of selections of prose and poetry, serious, humorous, pathetic, patriotic, and dramatic, for readings and recitations, than is Mr. Baker; for he is a practical elocutionist of high abilities, and from a boy has been a moving spirit in reading and dramatic clubs, and has written a large number of successful plays and dramatic poems. — *Home Journal.*

Sold by all booksellers and publishers, and sent by mail, postpaid, on receipt of price.

LEE & SHEPARD, Publishers, Boston.

You will find one of your Favorites among 50 of the Choicest
Selections in the

No. 2 Reading Club and Handy Speaker.

Edited by GEORGE M. BAKER.

Price, cloth, 50 cents; paper, 15 cents.

CONTENTS.

LEE & SHEPARD, Publishers, Boston.

You will find the Piece you are looking for among 50 of the Choicest
Selections in the

No.3 Reading Club and Handy Speaker.

Edited by GEORGE M. BAKER.

Price, cloth, 50 cents; paper, 15 cents.

CONTENTS.

"This is one of those books that our teachers ought to have at hand to *spice up* with now and then. This is No. 3 of the series, and they are all brim-full of short articles, serious, humorous, pathetic, patriotic, and dramatic. Send and get one, and you will be sure to get the rest." — *St. Louis Journal of Education,* January, 1876.

Sold by all booksellers and newsdealers, and sent by mail, postpaid, on receipt of price.

LEE & SHEPARD, Publishers, Boston.